Tour of Spain

Your Personal Travel Journal and

Adult Coloring Book

Location: 1 Tibidabo, Barcelona, Spain

C.A. Anderssen and Sophie Anders

THIS JOURNAL BELONGS TO:

_____

Cities Visited:

_____

_____

_____

_____

_____

Dates:

_____

_____

PRE-PLANNING
What to Pack (consider time of year & planned activities)

1. Medications

2. Toiletries

3. Passports / Travel Documents

4. _____

5. _____

6. _____

7. _____

8. _____

9. _____

10. _____

_____   _____

_____

_____

Location: 2 La Pedrera, Barcelona, Spain

ITINERARY

Dates, Destinations, Details

Travel Information

Flights, dates, restrictions, car rental/ transportation

_____

_____

_____

_____

Travel Agency Name & Number

_____

_____

_____

Travel Club Membership Info

_____

_____

_____

Travel Insurance Information
Policy #, agent name, company, etc.

_____

_____

_____

_____

Accommodation Information
Hotel, Address, Telephone, Confirmation #, etc.

_____

_____

_____

_____

_____

_____

Location: 3 Edificio Metrópolis, Madrid

Must See & Must Do

Helpful Translations

English	Spanish
1. Where is the restroom?	1. ¿Dónde está el baño?
2. Where is the train station?	2. ¿Dónde está la estación de tren?
3. I have a reservation...	3. Tengo una reserva ...
4. I would like to order...	4. Me gustaría ordenar ...
5. Please	5. Por favor
6. Thank you	6. Gracias
7. Excuse me	7. Disculpe
8. I'm sorry	8. Lo siento
9. Hello / Good Day / Good Afternoon / Good Evening / Good night	9. Hola / Buenos días / Buenas tardes / Buenas noches
10. Goodbye	10. Adiós

Other Phrases

Local Phrases
Region, Translation, How & when it is used

DURING MY VISIT
Day Trips & Events Planned

Favorite Food & Drinks
What is it? Where is it? History?

Favorite Places Visited

	New Friends
Name:	
Telephone:	
Email:	
Social Media:	
Address:	
How we met:	

New Friends	
Name:	
Telephone:	
Email:	
Social Media:	
Address:	
How we met:	

New Friends	
Name:	
Telephone:	
Email:	
Social Media:	
Address:	
How we met:	

New Friends	
Name:	
Telephone:	
Email:	
Social Media:	
Address:	
How we met:	

Location: 4 La Sagrada Familia

Location: 5 Park Güell

Location: 6 Alhambra

Location: 7 Ibiza

Location: 8 Casa Milà

Location: 12 Museo Nacional del Prado

Location: 14 Royal Alcázar of Seville

Location: 15 Gothic Quarter

Location: 17 Plaza Mayor

Location: 22 Plaza de España

Location: 25 Plaça de Catalunya

Location: 26 Alcazaba

Location: 28 Cathedral of Barcelona

Location: 29 La Giralda

Location: 30 Catedral de Sevilla

Location: 35 Ciutadella Park

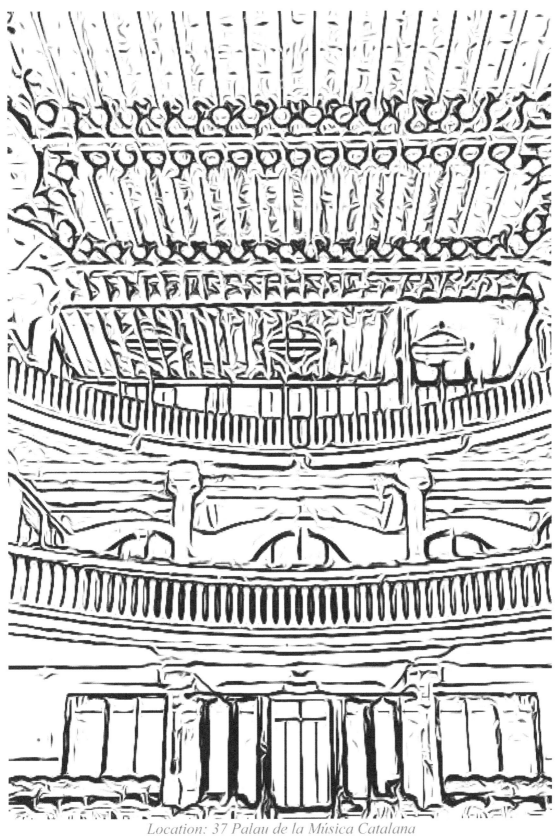

Location: 37 Palau de la Música Catalana

Location: 43 Picasso Museum Málaga

Location: 46 Güell Palace

Location: 49 Temple of Debod

Location: 50 Museu Nacional d'Art de Catalunya

Location: 52 Poble Espanyol

Location: 56 Tibidabo

Location: 63 Montjuïc Castle

Location: 70 Catedral de la Almudena

Location: 80 Santa Cruz, Seville

Location: 82 Casa Vicens Gaudi

Location: 83 Alcazar of the Christian Monarchs

Location: 84 Gaudi House Museum

Location: 85 Basilica of Santa Maria del Mar

Made in United States
Orlando, FL
29 November 2021

10893699R00065